New York City Haiku

Michelle Spadafore

Urban Ochre Press
Brooklyn, New York

Dedication

To my grandmother, Eleanor Spadafore.

"Traditional Japanese haiku have usually contained about seventeen *onji*. But an *onji* in Japanese is not the same thing as a syllable in English . . . In English haiku usually have fewer than seventeen syllables, though some poets do write them that way." William J. Higginson and Penny Harter, *The Haiku Handbook*.

"The guideline which has been followed the longest, and is by far the most important to the form, asserts that a haiku must be divided into two sections . . . For the purposes of this discussion, I would like to call the shorter portion 'the fragment,' and the longer portion, or two-line remainder of the poem, 'the phrase' . . . The fragment can be, or usually is, either in the first line or in the last one—either of the short lines." Jane Reichhold, *Writing and Enjoying Haiku*.

"Write [haiku] in three short lines using the principles of comparison, contrast, or association." Betty Drevniok, *Aware – a haiku primer*.

warm ramen shop
into cool night air
a solitary star

upturned face
covered in raindrops
broken umbrella

magnolia petals
already falling
dogwood arrives

late night heels
on cobblestones
no cabs

violently
blooming apple trees
heavy clouds

sprawled
by an empty newsstand
umbrella skeleton

faulty bulb flickers
all summer long
no fireflies

wonder wheel
silhouette on dark sky
lone balloon rises

hawks circle
on newly paved road
the sound of tires

faded roses in
flowered Sunday dress
old lady prunes

water lilies tense
on pool's surface
shadow glides below

bright umbrellas
waves cast up
broken seabird

winding
two hour line
five minute ferry

sunbathing
until the thunder
a mad dash

bugle sounds
on retired officers' porch
rocking chairs

honeysuckle rises
in the lightest passing
a door opens

busted radio
the highway stretches
to horizon mirage

iron storm clouds
air raid siren
sounds forlorn

solitary fishing rod
fisherman in icebox
misses the tug

Brecht in the park
absurdist plays
in 90-degree heat

white butterfly
drifting unnoticed
rapt audience

looking up
into the falling rain
time slows

chain link fence
thistles encroach
abandoned lot

low red sun
in concrete canyon walls
Manhattanhenge

retired schooner
worn sails sag empty
dry dock

overgrown churchyard
through rusted ironwork
a morning glory vine

ears perked puppy
awaits dog park entry
quivering

dawn calisthenics
waves against pilings
as seagulls alight

fishing poles slant
under Manhattan bridge
gulls wait watch

late night subway
workers hunch dozing
over heavy bags

wildflowers linger
small golden patch of
late September sun

missed turn
past silent warehouses
an unexpected vista

faded barges
tucked in narrow canal
water laps hollow

bright blue rope
cast upon rocky shore
clouds break

finishing a pastry
under close scrutiny
plump sparrows

dash down stairs
subway door
opens...closes

skateboards home
dry cleaning flapping
Williamsburg

steam rises
from morning coffee
bright pumpkins

autumn leaves
crunch under bike tires
red scarf flying

gold light pools
under arched streetlight
leaves slick asphalt

washed out sky
freshly shorn neck where
wool collar itches

a red wagon
filled with maple leaves
black branch above

orange halogen lamps
advance down misty road
scent of wood smoke

round sparrows cluster
around scattered seeds
frost on windshield

fingerless raglan gloves
wool collar turned up
blues played low

sunset reflects molten
off plate glass high rise
already night below

midnight cold
warm subway rumble
horn twice...passes

pristine white
shading to dark gray
day old snow

one trumpet flower
still on the vine
distant church bells

sax echoes
frayed velvet empty
train roars in

sardines on toast
step into misty dusk
halos of light

a bamboo forest
records shuffled in bins
overhead a bare bulb

gulls line pilings
river reflects dawn while
the tide rises

cobalt skies
with wisps of torn clouds
yellow leaves spinning

low morning sun
illuminates the last leaves
school bus rattles past

rushing rushing
cold wind on bare neck
shoelaces untied

garbage day
snow drifts within
empty circles

pale winter sun
orchid on windowsill
no buds

scent of dawn
beat cop clutches
bodega coffee

almost home
snow begins
horizontal

pigeons startle
in confusion of wings
snow crunches

cold radiator
three layers of clothes
and a hat

poblano peppers
in overwarm kitchen
onions caramelize

exhaust plumes
as engine warms
she waits inside

lead traceries
on a darkening sky
black branches

red green apples
with dusty sourdough
no more berries

fog muffles
a bar door opens
laughter escapes

intrepid ducks
the icy canal skin
marred by a v

scrape of bare twigs
scarf piled high but
shoulders hunched

oil pops in pan
sharp white cheddar
the fire alarm

pipe steams
icicles crash clang
off trash cans

washed out sky
backlit high above
a solitary bird

windows blacken
work day lengthens
4pm sunset

last night's dress
dawn breaks pale on
faded graffiti

hot dumplings
with every entrance
a burst of cold air

crunch of snow
freshly washed hair
icicle tipped

fog diffused lights
hazy reflections on canal
no moon

sea meets sky
gray shading to gray
lone surfer

leaving work
while still daylight
orchid blooms

wind gusts
frantic grab for
too loose hat

indigo sky
sparse clouds reflect
city lights

spring thunder
a flash diffused by clouds
subway roars underfoot

a plane ticket
from winter closet
sandals emerge

street cleaner whirs
a late thaw reveals
desiccated bicycles

Bushwick skyline
white curtains blow in
chill spring breeze

river captures dusk
the exact blue of the
Manhattan bridge

clear night
star studded sky
in frozen puddles

fortune cookies
just past new leaves
a crescent moon

removing vestibules
windows thrown wide
pansies on white linen

yellow flowers
late season rain
bows us both

magnolia blooms
scritch of ice scrapers
on windshields

now bareheaded
the streets fill quickly
April afternoon

spring!
overnight
daffodils

waves crash
dogs run joyful
off leash

taiko drums
cherry blossoms
fade into dusk

gold infused clouds
in humid honeyed air
rear window breeze

tan dust embeds
crisp white uniform
season opens

hazy sunlight
at seaside vendor
melting ice cream

summer sand
still caught in the treads
a screen door slams

early blossoms
rain stripped
morning fog

twilight
startled by
white dogwoods

blue tiles dusty
awaiting summer
pool dreams

cracked teacup
steam mingles with
jasmine rice

overcast
outrunning...running
whoosh!

still night
in humid heavy air
distant thunder

young Flatbush fig
faded by desolate heat
ah! fleeting showers

snow recedes
on pale winter skin
freckles emerge

dueling kites
their lines entwine
kamikaze

charcoal on wind
above city rooftops
distant fireworks

late summer
as sunflowers sag
drone of bees

steel girders rise
water tower sentinels
cast shadows below

sunflower dark
in summer gloaming
firefly alights

light rims
gathered clouds
low red moon

construction workers
on clean office stairs
early breakfast

sugar skulls
on Día de los Muertos
low wicks gutter

pumpkins slump
in late November
gap toothed

wasps buzz
hot apple cider
not sharing

horns blare
susurration against
stark sky

unexpected sunshine
leaves crunch under
autumn boots

last green tomato
on summer vine
crushed gingko seeds

painted faces
glimpse in passing
harvest moon

luminous gingko
under halogen lamp
heavier coat

from dense fog
bare trees emerge
a distant shore

river mist
police patrol boat
red then blue

no harbor lights
on dark horizon
fog horn sounds

night train
matte black glass
reflects sleepers

Christmas trees
in others' windows
biting wind

hunting blinds
dot frozen inlet
cracks widen

pearlescent sky
shading to pink
dawn bird cries

crystal sharp lights
line both bridges
orange moon rises

red holly berries
sparrow tracks
in new snow

pigeons huddle
on windowsill
cat quivers

early January
tattered pine trees
line sidewalks

winter parka
opposite side parking
in pink slippers

unbroken silence
snow blankets path
cardinal alights

big dogs bound
into snow drifts
small dog shivers

wind tugs
the blare of
car horns

linear shadows
of bare branches
add round sparrow

thin dawn line
under leaden clouds
suits fill subways

birdseed scattered
on frozen ground
cacophony of wings

just dodging
cab splashed puddles
skyscrapers end in mist

on the equinox
one last blizzard
today snowdrops

lugging umbrella
under forecast advice
cerulean skies

fallen tulip petals
against vacant stems
deep purple irises

skyward
a young oak reaches
among gravestones

night leaves
under halogen
rustling

scudding clouds
peridot willow electric
then muted

thunderclouds mass
on bruised horizon
close drone of bees

skyline ablaze
crimson brake lights
in falling dusk

fireworks scraps eddy
against police barriers
gunpowder lingers

ferry horn sounds
a late night arrival
no porch light

lost shoes dangle
a plastic bag now
airborne dervish

pale chrysanthemums
moonlight filtered by
rain splattered glass

ABOUT THE AUTHOR

MICHELLE SPADAFORE was raised in Northern California, but fell in love with New York City and never looked back. She works as a legal services attorney providing assistance to individuals with disabilities. She lives in Brooklyn with her partner, a cat, and a large bookshelf.

www.ingramcontent.com/pod-product-compliance
Lightning Source LLC
Chambersburg PA
CBHW021346060726
47591CB00006B/2188